I Wonder Why

Stalactites Hang Down

and Other Questions About Caves

Jackie Gaff

KINGFISHER

KINGFISHER
222 Berkeley Street
Boston, Massachusetts 02116
www.houghtonmifflinbooks.com

First published in 2003
10 9 8 7 6 5 4 3 2 1

1TR/1202/SHEN/RNB(RNB)/126.6MA

LIBRARY OF CONGRESS CATALOGING-IN-PUBLICATION DATA
has been applied for.

ISBN 0-7534-5573-0

Series designer: David West Children's Books
Author: Jackie Gaff
Consultant: Keith Lye
Illustrations: Peter Dennis 30l; Chris Forsey 8/9,
    24/25, 28/29; Mike Lacey (SGA) 4/5, 10/11,
    14/15, 26/27; Edward Mortelmans 31r;
    Nicki Palin 30/31m; Terry Riley (SGA) 18/19,
    20/21; Mike Taylor (SGA) 6/7, 12/13, 16/17,
    22/23; Peter Wilkes (SGA) all cartoons

Printed in Taiwan

CONTENTS

What is a cave?

A cave is a natural hollow or crack in the ground that's big enough for a large animal, such as a human, to fit inside. Sometimes a cave is a single, roomlike space called a chamber. In other places many chambers are connected by passages. This is called a cave system.

Which is the biggest cave chamber?

● With a depth of 5,598 ft., the Voronja (or Krubera) Cave in Georgia, east of the Black Sea, is the deepest cave explored so far.

The record holder is the Sarawak Chamber in the Gunung Mulu National Park, in the Malaysian region of Sarawak on the island of Borneo. It's a massive 3,292 ft. (700m) long, 1,359 ft. (415m) wide, and 262 ft. (80m) high.

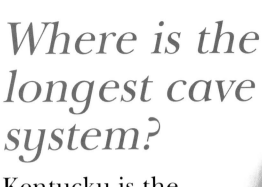

Where is the longest cave system?

Kentucky is the home of the world's longest-known cave system. It's called Mammoth Cave, and so far explorers have mapped around 353 mi. (570km) of passages. Believe it or not, people think hundreds more miles could be waiting to be discovered!

● There's enough room inside the Sarawak Chamber to park 40 airplanes.

How do caves form?

Most caves form in a hard type of rock called limestone as it is slowly dissolved, or eaten away, by acidic water. As rainwater falls through the air and down into the soil, it collects tiny amounts of the gas carbon dioxide. This gas mixes with the rainwater and makes a weak acid that is similar to the fizz in soda. As the acidic water trickles down through tiny cracks, it slowly wears away the limestone and eventually carves out chambers and passages.

● Around 13 percent of all rainwater ends up underground.

● Cave systems can contain streams, rivers, and even lakes and waterfalls.

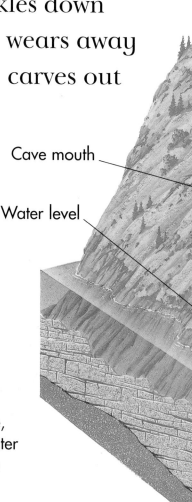

Cave mouth

Water level

● When streams or rivers flow through a cave, the sand and gravel carried by the rushing water scrape at the rock like sandpaper, wearing the rock away and making the cave bigger.

● Vertical cave passages are called chimneys or potholes.

● A basinlike opening called a sinkhole can form on the surface if the roof of a cave collapses.

● Large horizontal passages are called galleries.

Sinkhole

River

Gallery

Chimney

Waterfall

Lake

● One of the highest underground waterfalls is Ruby Falls in Tennessee. It plummets an incredible 144 ft.

What are stalactites and stalagmites?

Stalactites and stalagmites are spectacular, stony structures that can sometimes form inside limestone caves. Both structures are roughly carrot-shaped, but while stalactites hold tight to the cave roof, stalagmites are mounted on the cave floor.

● Stalactites and stalagmites can sometimes connect to make a column. One of the world's tallest is in Spain's Nerja Cave. It measures around 105 ft. from top to bottom.

Why do stalactites hang down?

As acidic water seeps downward it dissolves the mineral calcite, which makes up most of the limestone. When this liquid drips and dribbles from a cave roof, some of the water evaporates and changes into a gas, leaving some of the minerals behind as solids. Over time these minerals may grow downward to form stalactites.

Stalagmite

Stalactite

Column

Flowstone

- Stalactites never get as large as stalagmites. That's because when a stalactite gets very big, it becomes too heavy and crashes down from the cave roof.

Can you find fried eggs in caves?

You certainly can. Stalactites and stalagmites aren't the only amazing sights found in caves. Minerals can form all kinds of other weird and wonderful shapes and come in every color of the rainbow. In the Luray Caverns in Virginia there are two mineral formations that look just like fried eggs!

- Flowstone looks like a stone waterfall.

- Cave pearls can be the size of Ping-Pong™ balls.

Cave pearls

- Soda straws are hollow and look like the straws you sip drinks through. They are the beginning of a stalactite.

How do caves form inside icy glaciers?

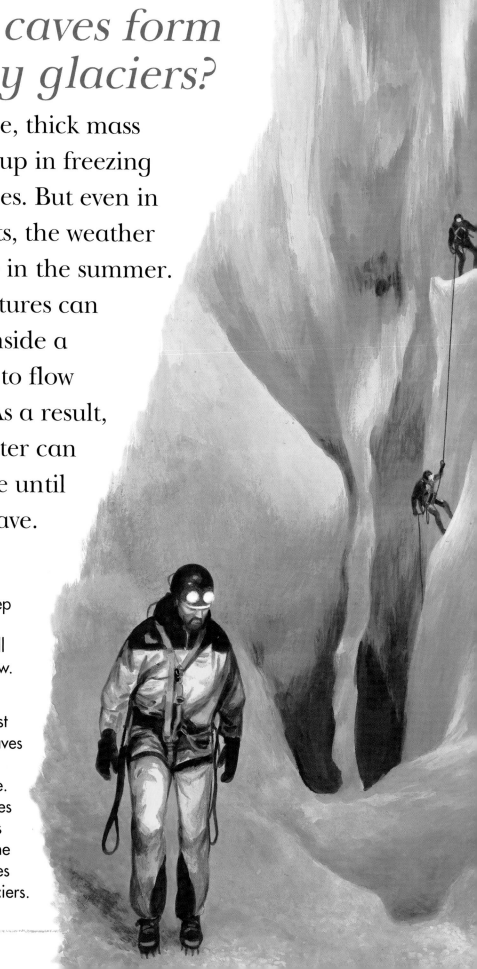

A glacier is a huge, thick mass of ice that builds up in freezing places like the poles. But even in the world's chilliest spots, the weather usually heats up a little in the summer. These warmer temperatures can make some of the ice inside a glacier melt and begin to flow away through cracks. As a result, the warmer, flowing water can melt more and more ice until it carves out a glacial cave.

● If a glacial cave isn't too deep below the surface, sunlight can filter down through the ice to fill the cave with an eerie blue glow.

● Some of the most stunning glacier caves are in Iceland, the land of ice and fire. Heat from volcanoes at the lowest edges of glaciers melts the ice, creating caves inside the glaciers.

Where is the "World of the Ice Giants"?

You'll have to take a trip to Austria to visit the "World of the Ice Giants," or *Eisriesenwelt,* the world's largest system of ice caves. Ice caves, unlike glacial caves, are formed when ice freezes on solid rock. The ice that coats the rock walls stays frozen all year-round.

● In parts of the "World of the Ice Giants" the ice is 65 ft. thick.

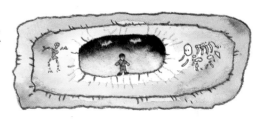

What is a lava tube?

It is a cave formed by lava—the hot, runny rock that pours out when a volcano blows its top. Sometimes, when lava flows downhill, its outer layers cool and harden into a solid crust, but its inner layers stay runny. If this runny lava drains away, a tubelike cave is left behind.

How does the sea scoop out caves?

Sea caves form along rocky coastlines as waves pound grit and pebbles against the land and make holes in the cliffs. Sea caves are often well hidden, with tiny entrances that are difficult to find and even harder to get to. It's one of the reasons why smugglers used to stash their loot inside them.

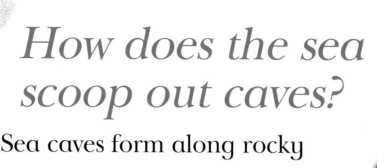

What is a blowhole?

Sometimes the power of a wave can smash a hole in a sea cave's roof. This opening is called a blowhole. When the seawater rises at high tide, waves pounding into the cave are squeezed up and squirt out of the blowhole like a giant fountain.

Where is the Blue Grotto?

The Blue Grotto is on the Italian island of Capri and is one of the world's most spectacular sea caves. It was named for the stunning sapphire-blue light that fills it on sunny days. The effect is created by the way sunshine filters through an underwater opening in the cave wall.

● An ancient boat landing step was found inside the Blue Grotto, proving that it was visited in Roman times.

Who wrote Fingal's Cave?

In 1829 the German composer Felix Mendelssohn was so inspired by his visit to Fingal's Cave that he named part of his Hebrides overture after it. The cave is on the tiny island of Staffa, off the west coast of Scotland.

Where would you find a spelunker?

Inside a cave, of course! Spelunkers are people who explore caves for fun. They are also known as cavers or potholers. Some spelunkers put on diving gear to explore flooded chambers and passages.

● Some cave passages are barely big enough for a spelunker's body.

What is the first rule of spelunking?

Never go inside a cave alone or without an experienced spelunker as your guide. Spelunkers always explore in groups. Caves are very dangerous places, and only trained spelunkers have the knowledge, experience, and equipment to explore them.

● Spelunkers protect themselves from jagged rocks by wearing helmets and heavy-duty clothing and shoes. They carry ropes and other climbing gear that help them climb up and down rock shafts.

Why do spelunkers wear lamps on their heads?

The deeper you go inside a cave, the darker, damper, and colder it gets. Spelunkers need lamps to help them find their way. Their lamps are on their helmets so their hands are free for climbing, crawling, and wriggling through narrow cave passages.

Where is the twilight zone?

A cave is a mini world of different light and temperature zones, with many different animals visiting or making their homes throughout. Some sunlight and rainfall reaches the entrance zone, and the temperature there is similar to the temperature outside. The twilight zone is darker, damper, and cooler. The dark zone of the inner cave is even cooler and wetter, and it's always pitch-black.

● The entrance zone—birds, such as cliff and cave swallows, often build nests on rocky ledges here, while insects and other creatures scurry around on the cave floor.

Can plants survive in caves?

You can sometimes find shade-loving plants, such as ferns and mosses, growing near the entrance to a cave, but green plants can't survive in the darkness of the twilight and dark zones.

● All living things need water, and even animals can't survive in the depths of a dry cave.

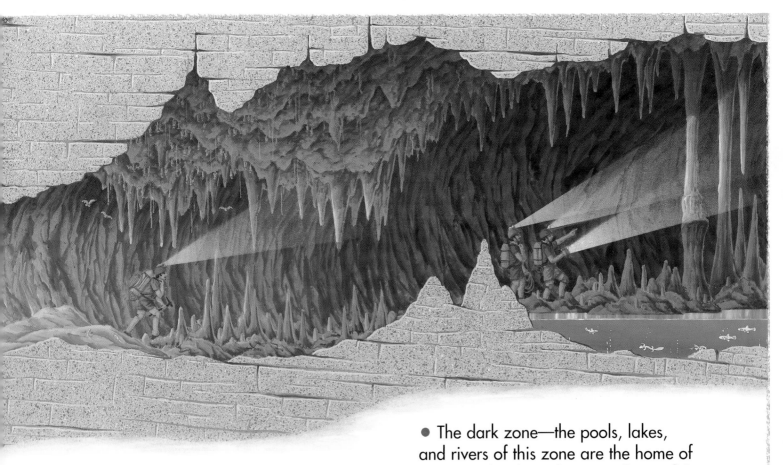

● The twilight zone—bats love to shelter here, as do snakes, some types of cave salamanders, and all kinds of cave creepy crawlies.

● The dark zone—the pools, lakes, and rivers of this zone are the home of strange, ghostly, pale types of cave fish, cave crayfish, and cave shrimps.

● Many different animals can live in a cave. For example, scientists have found more than 200 types of animals in Kentucky's Mammoth Cave.

Do mushrooms grow in caves?

Yes, they do. Mushrooms aren't plants, but they are a type of fungi—and fungi love the cool, damp, dark conditions inside caves. Bacteria, or germs, are another nonplant life-form that can survive away from light.

Do deer live in Deer Cave?

No, deer prefer forests to caves. Despite its name, Deer Cave in Sarawak's Gunung Mulu National Park is famous for its bats—around five million of them! Bats are night animals, and they like caves because they love the dark. They spend the daylight hours sleeping upside down, hanging from the cave roof. When dusk falls, they wake up and fly outside to hunt for their dinner.

● The record for the biggest bat colony is thought to belong to Bracken Cave in Texas. Around 20 million Mexican free-tailed bats spend part of the year there.

● Around 200,000 bats per minute stream out of Deer Cave at dusk!

How do bats hunt in the dark?

Although most bats have fairly good eyesight, this doesn't help them at night. Instead of relying on their eyes, bats use their ears. Each bat sends out a stream of high-pitched squeaks and then listens to the echoes made by the sounds bouncing back off of rocks, insects, and other objects. This technique is called echolocation, and it helps bats find their way, as well as track food, such as moths, in the dark.

● Some bats have a fold of skin called a nose-leaf on their snout. Scientists think the nose-leaf can be used to aim echolocation squeaks that help pinpoint a tasty target.

● Each bat sends out its own unique squeaks. These help each mother find her baby in a colony of millions of bats!

Which cave bird's nest is turned into soup?

Bird's nest soup is a Chinese delicacy— a food that is treasured in the East. It's made from the nests of swiftlets, a type of bird that lives in caves and uses echolocation. Instead of building their nests from twigs, the swiftlets weave them from their saliva, or spit, which cements the twigs to the cave wall.

● The nests are chewy but fairly tasteless, so flavorings, such as chicken stock, are used to liven up the soup.

● Removing the swiftlets' nests from a cave wall is one of the world's most dangerous jobs. Collectors climb incredible heights up bamboo poles to reach them.

Why do oilbirds go "click clack"?

Oilbirds also live in caves and use echolocation to find their way around in the dark. But unlike a bat's echolocation sounds, which are usually much too high for our ears to hear, an oilbird's are lower. An oilbird's echolocation noise sounds like the "click clack" of an old-fashioned typewriter!

Do bears live in caves?

● In North America other cave guests include pack rats, raccoons, and wildcats.

Bears will take shelter from the cold winter weather if they come across a cozy cave, but they don't live in caves all year-round. Like bats and birds, bears are cave guests, not cave dwellers.

● A cave dweller is an animal that spends its entire life inside a cave. A cave guest is an animal that visits a cave for part of the year for shelter or to hunt for food.

Which cave is lit up by insects?

There's no need to take a flashlight when you visit the magical Glowworm Grotto in New Zealand's Waitomo Cave. Its roof is lit up by thousands of tiny glowworms that sparkle and twinkle like tiny, blue Christmas tree lights.

● A famous New Zealand opera singer, Kiri Te Kanawa, once gave a concert in another part of the Waitomo Cave called the Cathedral.

Why are cave fish blind?

These fish are cave dwellers, and like other creatures that spend their entire lives deep underground, they don't need sight because they live in complete darkness. Instead of sight, cave fish have special nerve endings in their skin that help them "feel" their way around and track down food.

Cave fish

Which insects feed on bat droppings?

Bat droppings, or guano, are a rich source of food for tiny cave creatures such as cockroaches, flies, and millipedes. In turn, these creatures are snatched up by centipedes, crickets, and spiders, which are then hunted by larger cave animals such as bats and birds.

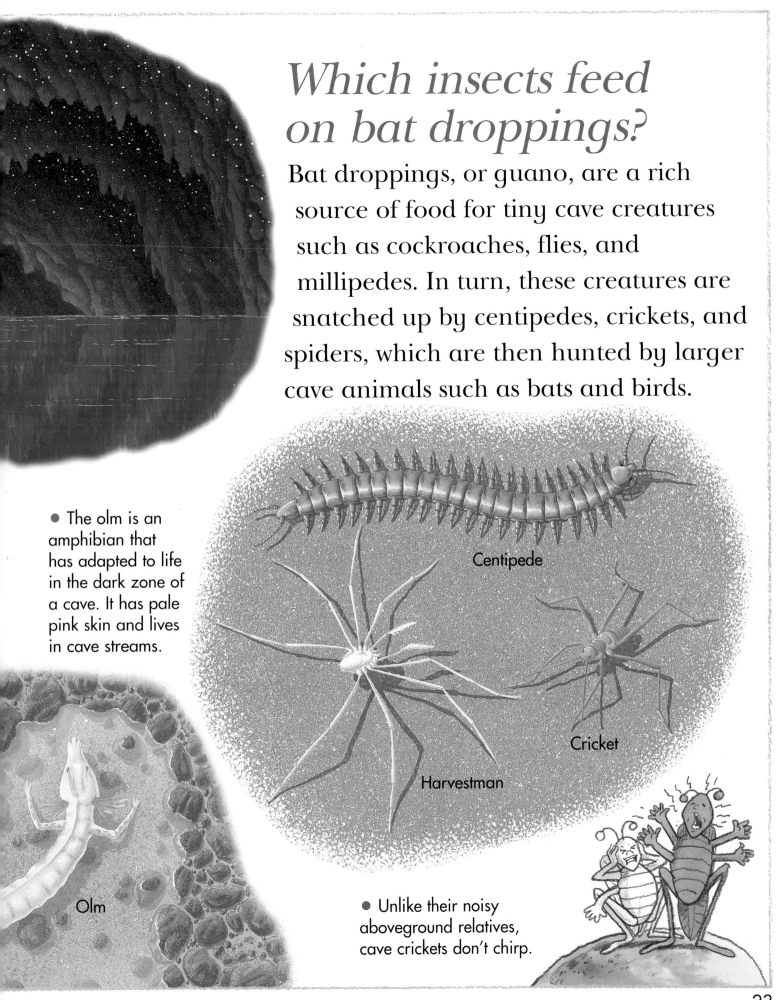

● The olm is an amphibian that has adapted to life in the dark zone of a cave. It has pale pink skin and lives in cave streams.

Centipede

Harvestman

Cricket

Olm

● Unlike their noisy aboveground relatives, cave crickets don't chirp.

What are the Lascaux Cave treasures?

Inside the Lascaux Cave in southwestern France there are ancient treasures that are much more precious than piles of glittering gold. The cave walls are covered with hundreds of lifelike paintings and carvings of animals—charging bulls, bison, musk ox, galloping horses, and leaping reindeer. The age of these magnificent pictures is even more astonishing—prehistoric artists began creating them around 17,000 years ago.

● The cave artists' yellow, red, and brown paint came from types of earth called ocher, while white came from clay or chalky stones. Black came from the charcoal of burned wood.

● Lascaux was discovered in 1940 by four boys on a walk. One story tells how they found their way into the cave by trying to rescue their dog after it fell in a hole.

● Cave artists painted with their fingers or with brushes made by attaching animal fur to sticks. Sometimes they blew paint through hollow bones—an early form of spray painting!

● Some of the images on the Lascaux walls are of animals that became extinct long ago and vanished from the earth—for example, mammoths and cave bears.

Who buried their dead in caves?

The ancient Egyptians are famous for building large pyramids, but there was a big drawback to these huge aboveground tombs. Every robber in the land could see exactly where the dead person's mummy and its treasures were buried. Around 3,500 years ago theft was such a big problem that the Egyptians came up with a new idea. They began carving secret cave tombs into the rock, where their dead could be hidden from the robbers' thieving hands.

● The walls of the cave tombs were decorated with beautiful paintings, many of them illustrating everyday life in ancient Egyptian times.

Which god did the Romans worship in caves?

One of the most important gods for Roman soldiers was Mithras, the god of light, who was portrayed slaying a bull in a cave. For this reason, soldiers worshiped Mithras in cave temples that they dug underground.

What are catacombs?

The ancient Egyptians weren't the only people to bury their dead in caves. Catacombs are cave tombs that Jews and early Christians began digging into soft rock under the city of Rome, Italy, almost 2,000 years ago.

● The Maraca people lived in Brazil, in South America, over 400 years ago. They made human-shaped urns from clay to hold the bodies of their dead and used natural caves as holy places to store the urns.

Where is the rose-red city in the rock?

● One of Petra's most magnificent buildings is a 131-ft.-high temple called the Khazneh.

Some ancient peoples carved entire cities underground or inside hills. Among the most famous is Petra in present-day Jordan. It is called the rose-red city because of the vivid color of its rock.

Do people live in caves today?

Yes, they do—either in natural caves or in rooms they've dug out of the rock. In the Shanxi Province of northern China, for example, millions of people live in cave homes. Some families even grow crops on their roofs.

● It's so hot during the summer that almost all of the buildings in the Australian mining town of Coober Pedy are underground. The town is a center for opal mining, and around 2,500 people live there.

Where can you play sports in a cave?

You can play hockey in Norway's Gjøvik Rock Cavern, which was blasted from the rock to house a huge underground sports stadium where hockey games were held during the 1994 Winter Olympics. At 298 ft. (91m) long and 200 ft. (61m) wide, it's one of the world's largest artificial rock chambers.

● Saumur, in France's Loire Valley, is famous for its cave homes. The caves were dug in the 1700s by stonemasons who used the stone to build the valley's great châteaus.

Why are caves good for cheese?

Caves are the key to one of France's most famous cheeses—Roquefort. It is made from sheep's milk, and its special flavor comes from streaks of bluish mold. Molds are fungi, like mushrooms, and they grow from seeds called spores. These are added to the sheep's milk at an early stage. The young cheeses are put in a network of caves, which provide the right climate for the spores to develop into mold.

● Cave conditions are also ideal for storing wine and for farming all types of edible mushrooms.

Which sun goddess hid in a cave?

When the Japanese sun goddess Amaterasu hid in a cave, the whole world was cast into darkness. Nothing would persuade her out until Uzume, the goddess of laughter, began dancing outside the cave. When Amaterasu sneaked a look, she was so fascinated by her own reflection in a magical mirror that she came out, restoring light to the world forever.

● The Zuni people of the southwestern U.S. believed that the first men and women were strange-looking creatures who came from four caves in the underworld. When they first came out of the caves, the god Yanauluha taught them how to grow plants and survive aboveground.

● The Maya people of South America believed in a cave-dwelling bat god called Zotz, who had the body of a human but the head and wings of a bat.

What is a troll?

In Viking and other Scandinavian legends trolls are scary creatures that are much bigger and stronger than humans. They live in caves and leave only after dark to hunt for their favorite meal—humans!

● In ancient Greek mythology a cyclops was a one-eyed giant who lived in caves and ate raw flesh, including that of humans.

Index